TRADITIONS AND CELEB

PRIDE MONTH

by Steve Foxe

PEBBLE
a capstone imprint

Published by Pebble, an imprint of Capstone
1710 Roe Crest Drive, North Mankato, Minnesota 56003
capstonepub.com

Library of Congress Cataloging-in-Publication Data is available on the Library of Congress website.

ISBN: 9780756576950 (hardcover)
ISBN: 9780756577315 (paperback)
ISBN: 9780756577322 (ebook PDF)

Summary: Pride Month is about celebrating the lives and activism of LGBTQ+ people around the world. It started as a way of remembering the 1969 Stonewall Uprising in New York City. During Pride Month, communities have festivals, parades, and marches. Some organize protests. Discover how people around the world celebrate Pride.

Editorial Credits
Editor: Ericka Smith; Designer: Kayla Rossow; Media Researcher: Svetlana Zhurkin; Production Specialist: Katy LaVigne

Image Credits
Getty Images: Jenny Evans, 27, Lauren DeCicca, 20, NY Daily News Archive, 6, Rebeca Figueiredo Amorim, 18, Redferns/Aldara Zarraoa, 25, Rodrigo Paiva, 19; Newscom: ZUMA Press/Rachel Adams, 23; Shutterstock: a katz, 13, Alessandro Biascioli, 4, Anna Fimina, 9, BeeZeePhoto, 1, DisobeyArt, 11, Eric Glenn, 5, Ivo Antonie de Rooij, 24, Kobby Dagan, 17, littlenySTOCK, 7, Lois GoBe, 22, Mario Hagen, 29, Patara, 21, Q Wang, 14, Rafal Kulik (background), back cover and throughout, Shawn Goldberg, 10, Svet foto, cover, 15, Wirestock Creators, 12

Printed and bound in China. 5593

TABLE OF CONTENTS

Words in **bold** are in the glossary.

WHAT IS PRIDE MONTH?

Rainbow flags hang from houses and store windows. Lesbian, gay, bisexual, **transgender**, and **queer** or **questioning** (LGBTQ+) people walk in **parades**. They organize **marches**. And they hold festivals. They're celebrating who they are. It's Pride Month!

Pride Month began as a way to remember the Stonewall Uprising. In 1969, LGBTQ+ people did not have many rights in the United States. They couldn't gather together. They couldn't marry each other either. What happened during the Stonewall Uprising helped change that.

People outside the Stonewall Inn during the 1969 Stonewall Uprising

On June 28, 1969, police **raided** a bar in New York City. It was called the Stonewall Inn. It was a meeting place for LGBTQ+ people. The police often raided LGBTQ+ meeting places. They would arrest queer people just for gathering together.

But people at the Stonewall Inn fought back that night. They were tired of being punished for who they were. The first Pride march was held one year later to remember the event—the Stonewall Uprising.

WHEN IS PRIDE MONTH?

Pride Month takes place in June in the United States. Many other countries hold Pride events during the same month.

Some places celebrate Pride during other months of the year. Australia holds its largest Pride events in February or March.

A Pride celebration in Australia in February

WHO CELEBRATES PRIDE MONTH?

LGBTQ+ people around the world celebrate Pride Month. They want to honor their identities and **advocate** for their rights.

Pride Month began as a protest. But the protests were a celebration too. LGBTQ+ people were happy to gather together. That made other people want to celebrate with them.

Today, many **allies** celebrate Pride Month too. Allies are people who support LGBTQ+ people. Allies might attend parades. They might donate to charities or volunteer at events.

HOW DO PEOPLE CELEBRATE PRIDE MONTH?

There are many ways to celebrate Pride Month. You can hang signs and flags to support LGBTQ+ people. You can honor LGBTQ+ activists and artists. You can also attend events.

UNITED STATES

Pride events take place all over the United States. The most common event is a Pride parade. During a Pride parade, LGBTQ+ groups walk or ride on floats through the streets. Some Pride parades are very small. Others are huge! They bring people in from all over.

All sorts of LGBTQ+ groups march in the parades. This includes sports teams, veterans, and drag performers. Drag performers dress up in fun outfits. Often they wear clothing intended for a different **gender**. They get the crowds excited.

Rainbow flags are very common at Pride parades. The rainbow flag was first created in 1978 to symbolize the LGBTQ+ community. Each color represents something different. Recently, the flag has changed to be more **inclusive** of transgender people and people of color.

The white, pink, and light blue stripes represent transgender people. The brown and black stripes were added to spotlight LGBTQ+ people of color.

As the site of the Stonewall Uprising, New York City holds a big Pride Month celebration. The NYC Pride March goes down the center of the city along Fifth Avenue. There are also concerts, boat parades, and parties.

San Francisco holds one of the largest Pride parades in the country. Nearly one million people attend it every year.

Los Angeles also hosts a large parade. In 1970, it was the first U.S. city to hold an official Pride parade.

A Pride parade in San Francisco

BRAZIL

The world's largest Pride parade takes place in São Paolo, Brazil. Brazil was one of the first countries in South America to give LGBTQ+ people legal rights. Brazil held its first Pride parade in 1997.

Now, more than three million people celebrate there every June. Pride has become one of Brazil's biggest tourist events. People in the parade often wear colorful costumes. The costumes have lots of feathers and glitter. It is common for famous people to appear in the parade.

ASIA

In some parts of Asia, LGBTQ+ people have only recently gained more rights. Because of this, Pride is celebrated in different ways across Asia.

In Thailand, there are huge parties. Visitors come from all over the world to dance all night.

People dancing during a Pride march in Bangkok, Thailand

In Japan, Pride is much smaller. That's because LGBTQ+ people in Japan are still fighting for more legal rights. It usually includes marches and speeches.

AFRICA AND THE MIDDLE EAST

Few Pride events take place in Africa or the Middle East. Many countries there still have laws against being queer. South Africa is the only country in Africa that holds an official Pride parade.

Celebrating Pride in Cape Town, South Africa

People attending a Pride event in Kampala, Uganda

But brave LGBTQ+ people in other African and Middle Eastern countries hold protests. Activists in Uganda have staged Pride events to protest unfair laws. Many have been arrested. Some have even been killed. Even though it is dangerous, they are keeping the original meaning of Pride alive.

EUROPE

The Netherlands holds an annual boat parade in its capital's canals. Thousands gather along the route to watch the colorful boats float by.

Spain hosts one of the largest Pride events in Europe. Every year, around two million people come to Madrid to celebrate. Madrid's Pride isn't just a party, though. The concerts and other events all support making life better for LGBTQ+ people around the world.

AUSTRALIA

Sydney, Australia, hosts WorldPride in February and March. The city also celebrates Gay and Lesbian Mardi Gras around the same time. This tradition began in 1978. That year LGBTQ+ people clashed with police in Sydney. They were fighting for their rights, like the people at the Stonewall Inn.

People celebrating Gay and Lesbian
Mardi Gras in Sydney

Whether large or small, Pride Month is a very important celebration for LGBTQ+ people. It honors the rights they have fought for. It is also a reminder of the advocacy for LGBTQ+ rights still needed around the world. Pride is a celebration of coming together as a community.

GLOSSARY

advocate (AD-vuh-kayt)—to support an idea or plan

ally (AL-eye)—a person united with another for a common purpose

gender (JEHN-dur)—a person's identity as a man, a woman, something between the two, or neither one

inclusive (in-KLEW-siv)—including all groups, especially those who have often not been included in the past

march (MARCH)—a group of people who walk together as an act of support or protest

parade (puh-RADE)—a line of people, bands, cars, and floats that travels through a town; parades celebrate special events and holidays

queer (KWEER)—holding an identity such as lesbian, gay, bisexual, pansexual, or transgender; identifying as something other than heterosexual or cisgender

questioning (KWES-chuhn-ing)—in the process of figuring out one's sexual or gender identity

raid (RAYD)—a sudden, surprise attack on a place

transgender (trans-JEHN-dur)—having a gender identity that does not match the sex assigned at birth

READ MORE

Clemesha, Chase. *People of Pride: 25 Great LGBTQ Americans*. North Mankato, MN: Capstone, 2021.

Gonzalez, Maribel Valdez. *Be Your True Self*. North Mankato, MN: Capstone, 2023.

Thor, Rosiee. *The Meaning of Pride*. Boston: Versify, 2022.

INTERNET SITES

Britannica Kids: Gay Pride
kids.britannica.com/students/article/Gay-Pride/634628

CBC Kids: Do You Know Your LGBTQ Flags?
cbc.ca/kids/articles/do-you-know-your-lgbtq-flags

Library of Congress: About LGBTQ Pride Month
loc.gov/lgbt-pride-month/about

INDEX

ABOUT THE AUTHOR

Steve Foxe is the Eisner and Ringo Award-nominated author of more than 75 comics and children's books including X-Men '92: House of XCII, Rainbow Bridge, Adventure Kingdom, and the Spider-Ham series from Scholastic. He has written for properties like Spider-Man, Pokémon, Mario, LEGO City, Batman, Justice League, Baby Shark, and many more. He is proud to help honor the many LGBTQ+ creators who have paved the way for him.